THE CATHOLIC
RUNNER

THE CATHOLIC RUNNER

30 DAYS OF MOTIVATION AND INSPIRATION

CHRIS EASTERLY

Our Sunday Visitor
Huntington, Indiana

Disclaimer: This book is not intended as a substitute for medical advice from physicians. The author is not a licensed medical provider, and author and publisher make no representation or warranties of any kind with respect to this book or its contents. The reader should consult with a physician before beginning any exercise program.

Except where noted, the Scripture citations used in this work are taken from the *Revised Standard Version of the Bible—Second Catholic Edition* (Ignatius Edition), copyright © 1965, 1966, 2006 National Council of the Churches of Christ in the United States of America. Used by permission. All rights reserved.

Every reasonable effort has been made to determine copyright holders of excerpted materials and to secure permissions as needed. If any copyrighted materials have been inadvertently used in this work without proper credit being given in one form or another, please notify Our Sunday Visitor in writing so that future printings of this work may be corrected accordingly.

Copyright © 2019 by Chris Easterly

28 27 26 25 24   2 3 4 5 6 7 8 9

All rights reserved. With the exception of short excerpts for critical reviews, no part of this work may be reproduced or transmitted in any form or by any means whatsoever without permission from the publisher. For more information, visit: www.osv.com/permissions.

Our Sunday Visitor Publishing Division
Our Sunday Visitor, Inc.
200 Noll Plaza
Huntington, IN 46750
1-800-348-2440

ISBN: 978-1-68192-410-6 (Inventory No. T2303)
1. SPORTS & RECREATION—Running & Jogging. 2. RELIGION—Christian Life—Inspirational.
3. RELIGION—Christianity—Catholic.

eISBN: 978-1-68192-411-3
LCCN: 2019949810

Cover design: Lindsey Riesen
Cover art: Shutterstock
Interior design: Amanda Falk

Printed in the United States of America

Contents

Getting Started — 7

1: Why We Run — 11
2: God Can't Steer a Parked Car — 15
3: Run Like a Child — 19
4: Run for Your Life — 23
5: Glorify God in Your Body — 27
6: When You Can, Do What You Can — 31
7: Fuel — 35
8: Rest — 39
9: Motivation — 45
10: Hills — 49
11: Aid Stations — 53
12: The Wall — 57
13: Between Heaven and Earth — 61
14: God Is a Runner, Too — 65
15: How Beautiful Are the Feet — 69
16: Run in the Night — 73
17: Run as Thanksgiving — 77
18: Run as Intercession — 81
19: Run as Service — 85
20: Run to Heal — 89

21: The Gift of Encouragement	93
22: Run with the Rain	97
23: Far More than All We Ask or Think	101
24: Run for Fun	105
25: Alien Race	109
26: Race Preparation	113
27: Phoenix Rising	117
28: Personal Best	121
29: We Never Run Alone	125
30: The Race Set before Us	129
Acknowledgments	133

Getting Started

Therefore, since we are surrounded by so great a cloud of witnesses, let us also lay aside every weight, and sin which clings so closely, and let us run with perseverance the race that is set before us, looking to Jesus the pioneer and perfecter of our faith, who for the joy that was set before him endured the cross, despising the shame, and is seated at the right hand of the throne of God.
Hebrews 12:1–2

I'm not a great runner. Sometimes I'm not even a good runner. But I am a runner, because I put on my shoes and start moving, whether it's down a neighborhood street, along a dusty trail, or around a cinder track. The great news is that anyone can be a runner.

Running is not expensive. (At least it doesn't have to be, unless you're into buying all the latest gear and gadgets like a heart monitor, a Garmin watch, high-tech clothing, gels, and other supplements.) All you really need to run is workout clothes and shoes. Some people don't even wear shoes, as evidenced by the brief barefoot running craze.

Running is not complicated. It's simple: one foot in front of the other. You can be fast or slow or anywhere in between. In contrast to basketball, baseball, or other sports, you don't have to learn a lot of rules, plays, and strategies. You just run. You can do it on a team or all by yourself.

Running is primal. Humans have always done it — they have run from predators, run into battle, run to deliver messages, run to relieve stress, or run to be in better health.

When I was six years old, my dad and brother and I would race each other in an elementary school parking lot. Each time, we staggered our starting positions: I, the smallest, was up front; my brother, four years older, a few yards behind me; and dad a few yards behind him. "On your mark, get set … go!" And off we went, shoes spitting gravel behind us. Of course, my dad and brother let me win. These "races" are some of the earliest memories I have of running, and they encouraged me to carry the practice into my adult life.

I've run 5Ks, half marathons, and one full marathon, but the greatest race I've ever run was into the arms of the Catholic Church. That race was more like a marathon than a sprint: I grew up Baptist but after nearly a decade of study, reflection, and prayer became Catholic in my thirties.

Catholics should integrate every part of our lives with our faith because God doesn't want us to compartmentalize. Our faith encourages us to strive for a healthy, holistic life in every aspect — spirituality, home, hobbies, work, physical activity, and everything else. As 1 Corinthians 10:31 says: "So, whether you eat or drink, or whatever you do, do all to the glory of God."

So it makes sense that the Faith should be an integral part of our experience as runners. That's where this book comes in. For the next thirty days, I encourage you to use *The Catholic Runner* to strengthen yourself as a runner and as a Catholic. Perhaps you are just starting out as a runner, and you want some advice and encouragement as you develop a new routine. Maybe you are preparing for a race; you can use this book to prepare, encourage, and inspire yourself, whether you start thirty days out or months ahead of the race. Or maybe you're a long-time runner who wants help delving into the spiritual fruit that can come from running.

Whatever your situation, I hope you will spend the next thirty days using this book to help you meet God in your runs and to allow him to encounter you there. In the following pages, we'll ponder what Scripture has to say about faith and running. Saint Paul, for example, made several great comparisons between the two (see the quote above). Throughout this thirty-day journey, you'll also read accounts of my own running experiences (like the time I ran a marathon while sick, or the time I raced alongside a bunch of pugs, or the time I ran through a torrential downpour in Southern California). Along the way, I'll share what I've learned about running and the spiritual life. I'll also provide quotes and insights from saints and runners much wiser than I am.

Whether you're a beginner or farther along in the life of running and faith, the race is set before you. So lace up your shoes, and let's get started!

1
Why We Run

*O God, you are my God, I seek you, my soul
thirsts for you; / my flesh faints for you, / as in
a dry and weary land where no water is.*

Psalm 63:1

REFLECT

It was around four forty-five in the morning, a quiet hour when much of the world is still dreaming. But I wasn't. For some reason, I couldn't sleep. Instead of lying awake staring blankly at the ceiling, I decided to go for a run.

I strapped on my Saucony Kinvaras, softly shut the door behind me so as not to disturb my sleeping wife, and headed outside. The Southern California air was dank, as if groggy from being up all night. I started down the sidewalk in front of my apartment building at a slow trot, then descended a hill and picked up my pace. After a half mile, I cut across the main road bisecting our San Dimas neighborhood and veered onto a residential street lined with houses. All the Craftsman homes were still dark, but the street lamps were on, spilling pools of light onto the asphalt, illuminating my path as I pushed myself up a hill.

The only sounds came from crickets and my own rhythmic breathing. My face was sweating, heart thumping, blood flowing. Endorphins exploded in my brain and rushed through my limbs. I was alive and aware of it, charged with the electric sense of presence that a good run can spark.

Why do we run? Ultramarathoner Bernd Heinrich wrote a whole book, *Why We Run: A Natural History*, to try to answer the question. He essentially suggests that it has to do with evolutionary biology: humans have evolved to run, just as birds have evolved to fly along certain migratory paths, or lions to track prey on the plains. That's probably part of it. In today's culture, maybe we also run to lose a few pounds. Or we enjoy the communal aspect of running with friends. Or we just like the way it makes us feel.

Why do we run? Maybe the better question is, Why don't we run?

For a variety of reasons, not everyone is a runner. But for

those to whom God has given the ability and the desire, the practice of running is a way to show our gratitude for that gift. We're taking care of our bodies so we can better serve our families and others, and live more productively the lives God has allowed us to live. Of course, running doesn't always feel like a gift. Some days it feels like a burden. We're tired and would rather kick back on the couch, eat chips, and stare at our phones.

But nobody ever wrote a motivational book called *Why We Eat Chips and Stare at Our Phones*. More importantly, when we give in to the siren song of the couch, we feel less alive, less right with ourselves and the world. When we settle for that lifestyle, we know deep down we're not living up to all that we can be.

Indeed, something elemental, something spiritual, occurs in the act of running. Whether we're aware of it or not, running gets us in touch with ourselves, God, and nature. I believe that's one of the many reasons why we run; we'll explore others throughout the next thirty days.

The answer to why we run cannot fully be put into words. Sometimes an answer can only be arrived at through doing. For me, running has a way of cracking open mysteries and revealing insights about myself, life, and the Divine. "I seek you, my soul thirsts for you; / my flesh faints for you," wrote King David. And I suspect that, on some level, that's why I got out of bed that morning and took off into the quiet dark. Maybe I simply couldn't sleep. But maybe something in me was seeking to connect with my Maker at the dawn of a new day.

Consider starting out this devotional — and your day — with a morning run. It doesn't have to be a predawn jaunt, but getting in a morning run, even if it's just ten minutes, is a good way to set the tone for the day, feel healthier, and maybe even encounter God.

PRAY
Lord, I consecrate to you all my thoughts, words, works, joys, and sufferings of this day — as reparation for my sins, to worship your adorable majesty, and to thank you for all your benefits.

RUN
Go for a run today. Move at an easy pace. If you are just starting out, try to go for a mile, and take it as slowly as you need to. If you're an experienced runner, go the distance that seems right for you. Notice how your body, mind, and spirit respond.

2

God Can't Steer a Parked Car

> *And I am sure that he who began a good work in you will bring it to completion at the day of Jesus Christ.*
>
> Philippians 1:6

REFLECT

Once, during college, I was struggling with a decision. I didn't know what direction to take, and I felt stuck. So I asked my mentor, an older Baptist preacher named Brother Ken, what to do. With a twinkle in his eye, he gave me this piece of advice: "God can't steer a parked car." Sometimes you just have to make a move and trust that God will take over, steering you where you need to go. Change will never happen until you start moving.

This is definitely true when it comes to running. We often

say we are going to start exercising and get in shape. But when the alarm clock beeps for our morning workout or the work day ends and it's time to hit the gym, we decide "Not today." We smack the alarm and roll back over or head straight home for dinner and some TV time before bed. We don't put on our running shoes and get out there.

Here's the simple truth: if you want to run — if you want to experience any positive change — you have to actually start running. So how do we get the car out of park? I use several strategies; maybe some (or all) of them will work for you.

Sometimes I'll go to bed in my workout clothes so that all I have to do when I wake up is put on my shoes and head out. I may feel tired, but usually the blood starts flowing and I'm alert once I get going. Before I know it, I'm a quarter mile down the road. Whether I end up running one mile or three miles that day, at least I've done something. Having pushed through my weariness, I feel much better for the rest of the day.

Another way to shift your car out of park is to schedule your run like any other daily appointment. If you commit to a lunch date, you typically make sure to show up. If you have a doctor's appointment or an important work meeting, you don't miss it. Treat your run the same way: schedule it, and make it a priority.

I've found it also helps to choose different running courses. Running the same route every day can get boring, chipping away at your motivation. Mix it up. Drive to a nearby park or the local

God Can't Steer a Parked Car **17**

high school track. Run on a paved course one day and a dirt trail the next. Treat yourself to some new scenery. Variety will spice up your run and keep you moving.

You can reward yourself for running. For every run you complete, treat yourself to something you enjoy. It could be a movie, a luxurious bath, a latte, or a small piece of chocolate. You probably shouldn't gorge on a giant ice cream sundae, because you'll just erase the health gains you made on your run. But a small, reasonable treat can be a good motivation to get you out and running.

You can also look at your run as an opportunity to learn something new. Instead of focusing on how tired you feel, notice your surroundings. Say "hi" to passersby. Learn the names of trees and flowers along your route. Listen to an audiobook or some good music. I recently discovered a screenwriting podcast I love, and now I look forward to my running time because it's a chance to spend thirty minutes catching up on it.

These are all strategies I use to make sure I get out there and run even when I don't feel like it. But no matter what trick I use to motivate myself on a given day, I usually find that while the new course, treat, or fun podcast may help the run go more quickly, it is not the reward. The run itself is the reward. I've done something good for myself, and I'm improving my health, and that feels pretty great.

So remember what Brother Ken said: "God can't steer a

parked car." If you feel the urge to start running, now is the time. Stop idling, shift the car into gear, and start moving. Employ whatever strategy helps you do that. You may have a glorious run, or it may feel like a slog. Either way, you're doing it, and that's what counts.

It takes your cooperation in getting yourself moving for God to begin a good work in you and bring it to completion.

PRAY
Dear God, help me shift my car out of park and get moving!

RUN
Use one of the listed strategies (or come up with your own) to motivate yourself to run today. Over the course of these thirty days, try out different motivators and learn which ones work best for you.

3
Run Like a Child

I praise you, for I am wondrously made.
Wonderful are your works!

Psalm 139:14

REFLECT

My parents took my brother to a football game when he was a toddler. While they were watching the game, he broke free and dashed out onto the fifty-yard line. My dad bolted after him and scooped him up off the field. The crowd cheered. My brother spoke his first words that day: "Let me go run!"

Running is innate for humans. From the earliest age, we have something inside us that instinctively longs to break free and bolt. Often, as we grow into adulthood, we lose this desire to run.

We get busy with our lives and grow sedentary. But I believe the instinctual desire to run is still there; if we revive and nurture it, we find that it never really went away. My brother, a retired army veteran, still goes on frequent seven-mile runs through the city or on wilderness trails.

The great thing about running is that you can do it at any age. It doesn't matter if you're nine or ninety. If you're in relatively good health, all you have to do is step outside or onto a treadmill. In 2011 in Toronto, a British man named Fauja Singh became the first centenarian to complete a marathon, crossing the finish line in just over eight hours. Singh credits the sport with giving him purpose and a sense of peace. "I don't stress," he said. "You never hear of anyone dying of happiness."

Indeed, running can contribute to your happiness, whether you're a toddler or a Sikh centenarian. It's a simple way that God has provided for us to stoke our sense of well-being. Physical activity produces endorphins, natural opioids that boost our mood. The interaction between physical activity, brain chemicals, mood, and the spirit is a fascinating mystery, one of God's many wonderful works. Why not take advantage of this natural antidepressant?

Running also keeps your body healthy and strong. According to a 2017 study published in the journal *Progress in Cardiovascular Disease*, running may be the single most effective exercise to increase life expectancy. That's because it combats common risk factors for early death such as heart attacks, high blood pressure, and excess fat.

Whatever your age, be careful to listen to your body so you don't overdo it. Consult your doctor before starting an exercise plan to make sure it's appropriate to your health. But know that you don't have to be a superior athlete to make running a habit or to reap its benefits. Running slowly is still running. Running shorter distances is still running.

And if you give running a try, you may just rediscover the childlike joy in it. Watch any kid running around a playground. It's not work for them; it's play. Any runner, at any age, can tap into that same sense of play. You may find that you want to do it rather than have to do it. You may find yourself shouting with my brother: "Let me go run!"

PRAY

Dear Lord, in you I live and move and have my being. Thank you that it's never too soon or too late to start running.

RUN

On your run today, try not to see it as work. Instead, focus on the joy of moving your body.

4
Run for Your Life

> *For as in one body we have many members, and*
> *all the members do not have the same function,*
> *so we, though many, are one body in Christ,*
> *and individually members of one another.*
>
> Romans 12:4–5

REFLECT

An alien spacecraft is firing lasers at hapless civilians. Or a giant mutant lizard is crashing through a densely populated city. Or a deadly meteor is rocketing toward Earth. "Run for your life!" shouts a character, and everyone flees in panic.

Hopefully, none of us will have to follow that wild-eyed

warning you hear in disaster movies. But the truth is that if you run, you actually are running for your life. Studies have shown that physical exercise, running in particular, can reduce mortality rates. Running for even five to ten minutes per day is associated with reduced risk of death from cardiovascular and other diseases. Moreover, running burns calories and helps you lose weight and maintain a healthy weight. It strengthens the heart, lungs, bones, and muscles. It's also good for the brain. It can reduce stress, improve memory and focus, and prevent cognitive decline. So whenever you run, you are indeed running for your life — to prolong it and to improve it.

Being physically and mentally fit positively impacts every other aspect of your life. You're sharper at work and stronger at play. Your thinking is clearer. You're also spiritually healthier. When you take care of the physical bodies God has given us, these "earthen vessels" (2 Cor 4:7), you are taking care of the home in which he lives.

Imagine if God showed up as a guest in your house. Would you want him to find a sloppy mess? Or would you want to welcome him into an inviting and well-ordered abode? None of us is perfect, of course. But God has given us the ability to take good care of ourselves. If, as Scripture says, our bodies are his temples (see 2 Cor 1:19), we should do what we can to maintain them well. We owe our loving Creator nothing less. And running is a great way to care for the temple he has given us.

But when you "run for your life," you're not just doing it for yourself. You're running for others' lives, too. Some of us are married, and some of us are single. Some have children, and some don't. But we all live in some kind of community — we have friends, siblings, parents, neighbors, coworkers who depend on us. No one is a complete lone wolf.

God said from the beginning: "It is not good that the man should be alone" (Gn 2:18). Instead, he created us to live with and for one another, as Paul told the Romans: "For as in one body we have many members, and all the members do not have the same function, so we, though many, are one body in Christ, and individually members of one another" (Rom 12:4–5). To some extent, we all have people who depend on us. When we run, we run for them, too. We want to be strong and healthy and available to help them in whatever way they happen to need us.

So the next time you lace up your running shoes, remember that you're running for your life — and others' lives, too. It's our obligation as brothers and sisters in Christ and members of the human family. It's a privilege from God. And it's our calling as the temples in which he dwells.

PRAY
Lord, help me exercise the privilege of maintaining my health, for myself and for those who need me.

RUN
On your run today, be mindful that you are not doing it just for yourself, but for others as well. Go online and find a local race that supports a charitable cause. Sign up and start training for it, to improve yourself and help others.

5
Glorify God in Your Body

So glorify God in your body.
1 Corinthians 6:20

REFLECT

Growing up in the Protestant tradition, I found my thinking informed by the notion that spiritual things are good, but the flesh is bad. After all, Saint Paul says: "For the desires of the flesh are against the Spirit, and the desires of the Spirit are against the flesh; for these are opposed to each other, to prevent you from doing what you would" (Gal 5:17).

Bible study, prayer, worship — these were all commendable. Anything focusing too much on the physical, however, was suspect. Taken to the extreme, this is a form of Gnosticism, a second-century heresy that claims that people are really spiritual beings trapped inside a human physical form. Gnosticism says that all matter is evil, while the spiritual realm is good. According to the Gnostic tradition, the goal of human life is to free ourselves from the body.

But John 1:14 says: "And the Word became flesh and dwelt among us, full of grace and truth." This is, in fact, the very heart of Christianity: when Christ was conceived in the womb of the Virgin Mary, God himself took on human flesh, proving that our flesh isn't evil, but rather very good. Human beings are not just spirits trapped inside bodies. We are spirits and bodies, and the parts cannot be separated from the whole. Indeed, Paul also writes that one day, our spirits and our bodies will be resurrected (see 1 Cor 15).

When I began to explore Catholicism, I started attending Mass occasionally. I was struck by how physical it is. All throughout the liturgy, Catholics use their bodies to worship. They dab holy water on their foreheads and inhale the scent of incense with their noses. They sit, they stand, they trace the Sign of the Cross over their heads and chests. They shake one another's hands as they offer the sign of peace. They kneel on bent knees as the priest holds up the Eucharist moments before they receive it in their open hands or on their tongues. The whole person, body and soul, worships God.

Something similar happens when we run. When consciously offered up to God, running becomes a form of worship; this happens in several ways. First, by exercising, we are being good stewards of the gift of physical health. We are taking care of, and improving, the bodies God entrusted to us. This in turn helps us become stronger, healthier, and more productive in other areas of our lives. We can have more energy to devote to our spouse and children. With clearer minds, we become better employees at work. We are more physically fit to serve our communities.

We also glorify the Lord with our bodies when we use them to do what they were designed to do. The sky glorifies God simply by being blue, gray, pink, or whatever color it happens to be at any moment. Water worships by flowing. Trees applaud in celebration as the wind rustles their leaves. "The mountains and the hills before you shall break forth into singing, / and all the trees of the field shall clap their hands" (Is 55:12). Nature praises God simply by doing what it was made to do. In the same way, we praise God with our bodies when we put them into action.

Jesus said that if the disciples were to be silent, then the very stones would cry out in praise (see Lk 19:40). But we don't have to leave it to the rocks. We can hit the road, put one foot in front of the other, and let our bodies do the praising. So when you go for a run today, offer it up to the One who made you to move. Glorify God in your body.

PRAY

Loving Creator, thank you for blessing me with the ability to move. I offer up my run as praise to you today.

RUN

Try adding an extra five minutes to your run today as you begin to prepare for your race. Offer it up as an act of worship.

6
When You Can, Do What You Can

> *For the sake of Christ, then, I am content with weaknesses, insults, hardships, persecutions, and calamities; for when I am weak, then I am strong.*
> 2 Corinthians 12:10

REFLECT

It was a crisp spring day. I was jogging around the paved loop in a local park, dodging worms and enjoying the scenery. As I rounded a bend, I saw a friend sitting on a rock reading a book. He called out my name, so I took a break to go chat with him. After a couple of minutes, I said I had to get back to my exercise.

"Sorry to interrupt your walk," he said.

My walk? I was running! Apparently, to him my slow shamble looked more like a leisurely stroll. Ego wounded, I shuffled back to the course and continued my run/walk. But it got me thinking: We don't always have to be the fastest. Running, after all, is simply putting one foot in front of the other in a forward trajectory.

In his book *Run Forever*, runner and coach Amby Burfoot says if you think you're running too slowly, then slow down even more. If that's how you can manage to keep moving forward, then do it without shame. After all, running is not about putting on a show, either for yourself or for someone else.

Maybe you're a beginning runner. Or maybe it's been a while since you ran and you're just starting again. That's okay. Move slowly if you have to. Some days, instead of an all-out run, you just need to "wog," as marathoner John Bingham puts it: walk-jog.

You may not resemble Usain Bolt blazing down the track, but you're still out there moving. Another way to say it might be this: run as though no one is watching. Because unless you're Usain Bolt, no one really is. Running is not about impressing others.

It's the same with the spiritual life. We can't always charge forward in an all-out sprint. We can try, but we'll inevitably burn out that way. Slow and steady wins the race, they say. Do you find it hard to pray for ten minutes? Then pray for five. Sometimes quality is better than quantity. As God himself said: "For I desire steadfast love and not sacrifice, the knowledge of God, rather than burnt offerings" (Hos 6:6).

It would be nice to sprint like a gazelle sometimes. But sometimes the best we can manage is a slow shuffle. And day after day of that slow shuffle will gradually condition us to run faster and pray harder.

And it may surprise you to learn that slowing to a walk during your run has benefits. Jeff Galloway, who popularized the Run-Walk-Run method, teaches that taking frequent walk breaks can actually improve your running pace. "Walk breaks will significantly speed up recovery because there is less damage to repair," Galloway advises. "The early walk breaks erase fatigue, and the later walk breaks will reduce or eliminate overuse muscle breakdown." Many runners have reported improving their race times by using this method.

So run slow. Run relaxed. Run happy. Try breaking up your run with frequent walk breaks. Unless you're a competitive athlete, running isn't a contest. My old Baptist preacher used to say: "When you can, do what you can. When you can't, take it easy." That's good advice, both for running and for the spiritual life.

PRAY
Lord, help me go at the pace that is best for me. When I can't go faster, help me take it easy.

RUN
Try breaking up your run with walk breaks today. Run for one minute, walk for thirty seconds, then run for one minute. Repeat until you've finished your workout. Plan to work this pattern into your training periodically throughout the rest of these thirty days to build up your speed and endurance.

7
Fuel

My flesh and my heart fail,
but God is the strength of my heart
and my portion forever.

Psalm 73:26

REFLECT

My whole body shivered, clammy and dehydrated, as I lay curled on the couch in my apartment. It wasn't winter, and I didn't have the flu. So how had I ended up in this miserable condition? It had all started a couple of hours earlier when I decided to go for a ten-mile run in the noonday heat — without food or water.

My first mistake was leaving my apartment just as the sun was reaching its zenith, the hottest time of day. It was a clear, beautiful Saturday, and it seemed like a good idea at the time. I left North Hollywood and ran down the long, urban sidewalk that stretches all the way to Burbank, five miles away. A couple of miles in, it occurred to me that I hadn't eaten breakfast ... and that I'd forgotten to bring a water bottle. Oh well. I was too far down the rabbit hole now, so I kept moving. By the time I passed beneath the giant mural of Superman outside the Warner Brothers studio lot, I was desperately smacking my dry lips for any trace of moisture to quench my parched throat. I was thirsty. So thirsty.

By the grace of God, I finally arrived at the halfway point: Bob Hope Park, a grassy island wedged between NBC Studios and the 134 freeway. The sun raged high in the Burbank sky, torturing me with its merciless ninety-degree rays. And then I saw it. Near a picnic table, a stone water fountain summoned me like a glorious mirage. I bolted toward the fountain, cranked the spigot, and gulped deeply of its refreshing elixir.

Momentarily bolstered, I wiped the water from my chin and pivoted back toward North Hollywood for the second half of my trek. Three miles later, I was dragging my feet and choking on my own desiccated trachea. I spotted a McDonald's up ahead. Unfortunately, I had also forgotten to bring my wallet, so I stumbled inside the restaurant's men's room, shut the door, and turned on the faucet. I lapped up the cool H_2O like a ravenous dog. Tap water had never tasted so good. Sun-baked and depleted, I walked the final two miles back to my apartment, staggered inside, and collapsed on the couch.

God designed our bodies to do amazing things, like run ten miles in the sun. Because they require energy to do these amazing things properly, he also provided that for us. Our bodies need carbohydrates and protein to power our physical activity. We need water to hydrate us along the way. Without this fuel, our bodies break down under the load and refuse to operate effectively.

When you set out on a run, don't forget to charge up first. Eat some fruit or maybe a slice of toast with almond butter, something to give you calories and energy for the physical demands ahead. Bring a bottle of water to keep yourself hydrated. The run won't always be easy, but you'll have the proper strength to complete it.

Just as we need physical fuel to run, we need spiritual fuel to live the Christian life. Jesus said: "Whoever drinks of the water that I shall give him will never thirst; the water that I shall give him will become in him a spring of water welling up to eternal life" (Jn 4:14). I could have used a literal spring of water that day in Burbank. But Jesus, of course, is talking about the life of the spirit. If we set out spiritually unprepared, the metaphorical sun becomes too hot, our spirits fail, and we end up shuffling the last few miles home, broken and defeated in the spirit.

To live the Christian life well, serving God and others, nourish yourself on the insights, strength, and wisdom of Scripture. Let the Holy Spirit fill you in prayer. Feed on the Eucharist to provide strength for your journey. Stay close to the living water. Then you'll be able to finish the race strong, whether that's a mission trip to a foreign land, serving at a local soup kitchen, or faithfully living out the family and work obligations of a normal day. Properly fueled, you'll be able to say with Saint Paul: "I have fought the good fight, I have finished the race, I have kept the faith" (2 Tm 4:7).

PRAY
Lord, help me always to fuel myself properly, in both body and spirit.

RUN
Before your run today, consume a small amount of carbs and protein. Bring along some water to keep you properly hydrated. Many sporting goods stores sell water bottles that strap to your hand or attach to a belt as you run.

8
Rest

*Come to me, all who labor and are heavy laden,
and I will give you rest. Take my yoke upon you,
and learn from me, for I am gentle and lowly
in heart, and you will find rest for your souls.
For my yoke is easy, and my burden is light.*

Matthew 11:28–30

REFLECT

Believe it or not, you can become a better runner by not running … sometimes. It's true that in order to improve our fitness, we have to put in regular time training. But we also need rest.

If you're training seriously for a race, you may balk at the thought of skipping a workout. However, rest is crucial for recovery and improvement. Think of rest days as simply part of your overall workout routine.

Whenever we run, the impact creates microscopic tears in our muscle fibers. Rest allows these fibers to repair themselves, making us stronger. If we continually stress our muscles without letting them rest, they have no chance to heal, and we can't reap the benefits of all our hard work. Even worse, we risk injury. Running strengthens bones by forcing them to remodel with a stronger structure. But too much repeated impact can cause stress fractures — small cracks in the surface of the bone. Proper rest gives the bones time to heal.

It sounds counterintuitive, but taking a break every few days will make you a better runner. On nonrunning days, try an alternative exercise that works different muscles. You could go for a low-impact bike ride or a swim, or lift weights. Or you could just spend the day off doing some other activity you enjoy. Take a nap. Read a book. See a movie.

Taking a brief break from running also refreshes you mentally. Running can become monotonous if you never give yourself a break from it. Often, a rest day is just what your mind needs to stay in the game. Then you can return to running the next day, reinvigorated mentally and physically.

Our need for rest extends far beyond our running routine. God built a rest day into the week. After a six-day world-creating marathon, he took a break. "And on the seventh day God finished his work which he had done, and he rested on the seventh day from all his work which he had done. So God blessed the seventh day and hallowed it, because on it God rested from all his work which he had done in creation" (Gn 2:2–3). Why did God rest? Certainly not because he was tired: God's energy is inexhaustible, constantly sustaining the entire universe. Maybe he rested so he could simply enjoy the goodness of what he had created.

The *Catechism of the Catholic Church* says: "God's action is the model for human action. If God 'rested and was refreshed' on the seventh day, man too ought to 'rest' and should let others, especially the poor, 'be refreshed.' The sabbath brings everyday work to a halt and provides a respite. It is a day of protest against the servitude of work and the worship of money" (CCC 2172).

God appointed the seventh day (*Shabbat* in Hebrew, meaning "to rest from labor") as a day of repose for his people. Apparently, he knew we needed an occasional break. God's people were to honor him on that day by ceasing from their daily labors and celebrating him in worship. Jews and Christians are still called to recognize the Sabbath by resting.

The rest God provides can be more than a break from physical activity. Jesus said: "Come to me, all who labor and are heavy laden, and I will give you rest. Take my yoke upon you, and learn from me, for I am gentle and lowly in heart, and you will find rest for your souls. For my yoke is easy, and my burden is light" (Mt

11:28–30). What does this mean?

Often in life, we can feel like an ox dragging along a heavy burden. Our minds are troubled, and our hearts are anxious. But Jesus says that if we learn from him, we can experience a wonderful spiritual peace, even in the midst of life's troubles. Drawing close to Jesus in prayer, Scripture, and the sacraments lightens our spiritual load and allows our souls to rest. Saint John Paul II said: "There is no evil to be faced that Christ does not face with us. There is no enemy that Christ has not already conquered. There is no cross to bear that Christ has not already borne for us, and does not now bear with us."

Spiritual respite and refreshment are available to all who follow Jesus. There is also an eternal rest, which the Letter to the Hebrews describes: "So then, there remains a sabbath rest for the people of God; for whoever enters God's rest also ceases from his labors as God did from his. Let us therefore strive to enter that rest, that no one fall by the same sort of disobedience" (Heb 4:9–11).

One day, after we persevere, God's children will enter into that blessed rest. While we remain in this life, though, we need to take advantage of periods of rest, and this includes resting from our runs. So run well. But rest well, too.

PRAY
Lord, help us know when to run and when to rest.

RUN
Depending on your energy levels, take a rest day or two from running this week. On your rest days, try a different form of exercise or simply relax and give your body a chance to heal and restore.

9
Motivation

*Let no evil talk come out of your mouths, but only
such as is good for edifying, as fits the occasion,
that it may impart grace to those who hear.*
                                        Ephesians 4:29

REFLECT

Running is as much a mental activity as a physical one. When the mind and the body cooperate, we can often accomplish more than we thought possible. Encouraging yourself with short phrases and slogans can motivate you to push through challenges and difficulties.

In our Catholic tradition, we often motivate ourselves to do tough things through aspirations — short prayers, Scripture verses, or quotes from saints that we can repeat to keep ourselves moving toward a goal. More than a nice spiritual practice, this is deeply rooted in our psychology as human beings. Our thinking informs and determines our actions; often, in order to change our thinking, we have to tell ourselves the truth about what we're capable of. A few small words can help the mind push the body past its perceived limits.

Aspirations and other forms of self-motivation can be incredibly helpful for us as Catholic runners. Typically, they work best when they are short, succinct, and easy to remember. There is no limit to the prayers, Scripture verses, and quotes from saints that you can employ to encourage yourself as you run. Use whatever helps. As Catholics, we can draw from a great wealth of motivation that is good not just for our physical fortitude but for our souls as well. Here are just a few examples:

Scripture Verses
- But they who wait for the Lord shall renew their strength,
  they shall mount up with wings like eagles,
  they shall run and not be weary,
  they shall walk and not faint. (Is 40:31)
- I do not run aimlessly, I do not box as one beating the air. (1 Cor 9:26)
- But Jesus looked at them and said to them,

> "With men this is impossible, but with God all things are possible." (Mt 19:26)
- I can do all things in him who strengthens me. (Phil 4:13)
- I am with you always. (Mt 28:20)

Quotes from Saints
- Pray, hope, and don't worry. (Saint Pio of Pietrelcina)
- If you have God as the center of all your action, you will reach your goal. (Blessed Pier Giorgio Frassati)
- We cannot all do great things. But we can do small things with great love. (Saint Teresa of Calcutta)

You might also choose to use a short, simple prayer. For instance, when striving to finish a grueling workout, I sometimes utter the simple phrase "Jesus, help." This is a powerful prayer, whether uttered during the final lap of a run or in a difficult life circumstance. When you're facing either, find the best encouraging quotes and prayers to help you push through.

PRAY
Lord, provide me all the motivation I need to become a better runner and a stronger Christian.

RUN
Pick one of the quotes or prayers above (or choose your own), and practice repeating it during your run today.

10
Hills

Every valley shall be lifted up, and every mountain and hill be made low.

Isaiah 40:4

REFLECT

I love running on flat courses. Who doesn't? Your legs are not as strained, your lungs are less taxed, and you can generally go faster. But run long enough, and eventually you'll encounter hills.

Some runners love hills. Some dread them. Either way, hills are good for us. They force us to dig deeper and push ourselves harder. This is good for us, both mentally and physically. Running up inclines burns more calories, helping you shed weight. The steeper the hill, the more calories burned. The less body weight you carry, the more efficiently you can run.

Running hills works your calves, quadriceps, hamstrings, and glutes. It also strengthens tendons, which can help prevent injury. Building muscle strength improves your speed. You may curse the hill as you're tackling it, but the effort you're expending will help you run faster when you're back on a flatter surface. After several days or weeks of running hills, you'll be surprised at how effortless running on a flat course can feel.

The strength and speed you develop from running inclines will also boost your confidence. After training on hills during your workouts, you'll be better mentally prepared to handle them when you encounter them during a race. You'll also enjoy the satisfying feeling of accomplishment when you reach the top.

Then, of course, you get to enjoy running down the other side of the hill — but you have to be careful here. You can't just fly down the slope, because running downhill engages the muscles differently. The downward stride results in more ground reaction force, increasing your impact, which can stress your bones and muscles, especially the hip flexors. Here is a bit of advice, runner to runner: Running downhill smartly is just as important as running uphill. When descending a hill, resist the urge to lean back, which may cause more stress from impact. Lean forward at the hips instead of at the shoulders, but be careful not to lean too far forward, or you risk falling over. Gravity will do a lot of the work. Take the decline more slowly, and use your arms for balance.

If you have never trained on hills, ease your way into it. Don't try to attack a super-steep incline right away; you'll just run out of breath, trash your legs, and become discouraged. Start with smaller hills, repeating several of these at first. After you've acclimated to running up smaller inclines, try steeper ones. Over time, you'll build your fitness and ability to handle hills. If you don't live in a hilly area or you can't exercise outside, running on a treadmill works, too. Set the machine at an incline to enjoy the same benefits as running up a hill. Running stairs is a good option, as well.

As with most things running, learning to embrace and conquer hills can prepare you for other challenges in life. Are you facing a daunting project at work? Dealing with a difficult personal relationship? Maybe life in general just feels like an uphill battle at the moment. The mental strength and confidence you develop from running hills can help you tackle these trials.

The same holds true for the spiritual hills we encounter. When we bravely face one of these inclines — whether it's ministry stress, dryness in prayer, doubts, or another challenge that tests our faith — and find that we have overcome it with God's grace, our faith is strengthened, and we are stronger for the next one. Like it or not, we will inevitably face these hills in our spiritual journey. But this is good; they are the only way we can grow stronger.

So when you encounter hills on your run or in your spiritual life, try not to fear them. Embrace them, and let them strengthen you. They will make you a better runner and a stronger person.

PRAY
Lord, help me not to be afraid of hills, whether they rise up on a run or in my spiritual life. Instead, help me use them to grow stronger.

RUN
Try mixing up your run today by adding one or two inclines. Start with smaller hills, then gradually attempt steeper inclines. If you don't have access to real hills, use the incline setting on a treadmill.

11
Aid Stations

I am the vine, you are the branches. He who abides in me, and I in him, he it is that bears much fruit, for apart from me you can do nothing.

John 15:5

REFLECT

Maybe you are running a 5K, or maybe it's an ultramarathon. But every two to three miles, you will encounter them: blessed aid stations, oases of refreshment in the midst of your race. The aid station is typically a table staffed by volunteers ready to hand you a tiny paper cup of water or Gatorade. Maybe there are orange slices and salt packets too, to restore the electrolytes you've depleted so far. Runners need aid stations. Can you imagine running a race without any help along the way?

I always slow down to a walk at aid stations and take the cup of water from the volunteer, whom I make sure to thank. As I walk, I swig down the water, crush the cup, and toss it in the trash can that's usually there on the side of the course. Then I pick my pace back up and resume running.

Merriam-Webster.com defines a station as "a regular stopping place in a transportation route." Aid stations are good for runners, physically and mentally. They remind us we are not superhuman, that we can't continue the race without a little help. Nobody can run a 10K, let alone a marathon, without hydrating along the way. Aid stations are also a reminder that we are not alone — someone has thought to be there for us and help us out on the journey.

For Catholics, the Church is the ultimate aid station. In life's daily race, we often get depleted and weary. We need to refuel and nourish ourselves for the journey ahead. To continue running the race, we need sustenance now. The Church meets our immediate need, enabling us to continue our spiritual race. Otherwise, we will lose strength and not be able to finish. The Church is not a bastion of champions, but a way station for all those running the race and finding themselves in need of support along the way.

Even Jesus, during his Passion, needed help to continue. The traditional Stations of the Cross devotion depicts fourteen key moments of Christ's path to his crucifixion. Especially during the season of Lent, Catholics all over the world reenact and meditate on these stations to commemorate Christ's sacrifice for us. In the sixth station, we meditate on a woman named Veronica, who sees Jesus carrying his cross and feels sympathy for him. She wipes his face with her veil, and he leaves an image of his face on the cloth as a way to show his thanks. Veronica was Christ's aid station along the Way of the Cross.

We often stumble along life's race thinking we can do it all on our own. But we all need help. Scripture confirms this: "Two are better than one, because they have a good reward for their toil. For if they fall, one will lift up his fellow; but woe to him who is alone when he falls and has not another to lift him up" (Eccl 4:9–10).

If Christ himself needed aid to complete his journey, then so do we; Jesus himself said: "A servant is not greater than his master" (Jn 15:20). Therefore, we should take advantage of all the aid the Church offers as we run our spiritual race. After all, Jesus reminds us that he is the vine and we are the branches; apart from him, we can do nothing (see Jn 15:5). Both in your running and in life, never try to go it alone. Accept help. Receive nourishment. It's the only way you will complete the race.

PRAY
God, give me the wisdom and humility to seek out and receive aid when I need it.

RUN
If you've signed up for a local race, make sure to seek advice and help from others as you prepare. During the race, plan to take advantage of the aid stations, and thank the volunteers for their help.

12
The Wall

*Yes, by you I can crush a troop; and by
my God I can leap over a wall.*

Psalm 18:29

REFLECT

In marathons, it typically happens between miles 15 and 20. You're running along fine, when suddenly your body wants to come to a screeching halt. You can't go on. You've hit "the wall." Anyone who's run long distances for a while knows this miserable feeling well. The wall is not just physical; it impacts our mental state, too. We feel grumpy and dejected, our brain cluttered with negative thoughts.

Why does this happen? During long-distance exercise, our

bodies produce energy in two ways. First, they tap into fat stores. Next, they access glycogen, the primary carbohydrate stored in the liver and muscles. Many runners load up on carbohydrates a few days before a long-distance race, devouring complex carbs like pasta, rice, whole grains, and potatoes. This ensures that glycogen levels are maximized before the big event. Glycogen is broken down into glucose, which provides the body with a readily available source of energy. When glycogen is depleted, the body runs out of energy, and the person crashes into the wall. Runners know that when this happens, they must replenish their glycogen stores in order to go on.

If you hit the wall during a run, how do you push through it? One strategy is simply to reduce the intensity of the exercise. Slow down. But ultimately, it's imperative to replenish your glycogen stores. You can down an energy drink or eat a carb-rich snack. Many runners also consume supplements like a GU gel packet or sports jelly beans. These are all ways of raising your glucose levels and keeping you going. Most healthy runners can exercise for around two continuous hours before glycogen reserves must be replenished. In his book *Ultramarathon Man*, Dean Karnazes recounts one long-distance run when he actually ordered a pizza and had it delivered to him on the side of the road! Whatever works.

Hitting — and overcoming — the wall holds lessons for us not just in running, but in every area of our lives. We all occasionally hit physical, spiritual, emotional, or circumstantial walls in life. When this happens, we become depleted and feel like we can't go on. We must break through these walls the same way an athlete does, by restoring our energy reserves. As Catholics, we do this by partaking of the sacraments, especially Reconciliation and the Holy Eucharist.

When we neglect our spiritual health and fall into sin, we need to be restored. Going to confession provides this restoration. After we make an honest confession, we are absolved of our sins and strengthened spiritually to continue the race. Jesus told the woman caught in adultery: "Neither do I condemn you; go, and do not sin again" (Jn 8:11).

Upon receiving the Body and Blood of Christ in the Eucharist, we are infused with spiritual power to keep living the Christian life. We are empowered by the very presence and closeness of God to press on and keep running the daily race set before us. Christ promised us: "He who eats my flesh and drinks my blood abides in me, and I in him. As the living Father sent me, and I live because of the Father, so he who eats me will live because of me" (Jn 6:56–57).

The Church teaches that the sacraments dispense divine life and power to those who receive them in faith. Recall the story from the Gospel of Luke in which Jesus heals a woman afflicted with a hemorrhage. She reaches out and touches the hem of Jesus' cloak, and Jesus tells her: "Daughter, your faith has made you well; go in peace" (Lk 8:48).

When we partake of the sacraments, we, like the woman with the hemorrhage, are touching the hem of Jesus' cloak, allowing his power to wash over us and restore our spiritual fuel reserves. This enables us to leap over the walls that life puts in our way.

PRAY
Lord, let me always turn to you to receive the strength I need to break through walls.

RUN
On your run today, pay attention to when your body seems to hit the wall. Rather than giving in and quitting, see if you can press on. Bring along a small snack so that, if you hit the wall, you can slow down, refuel, and continue.

13

Between Heaven and Earth

Every good endowment and every perfect gift is from above, coming down from the Father of lights with whom there is no variation or shadow due to change.

James 1:17

REFLECT

While every distance runner knows the wall all too well, another feeling that runners encounter makes the wall absolutely worth it. Any runner who's been doing it long enough has experienced this feeling — that sublime moment when you mysteriously seem to transcend the physical. Your bodily effort ceases to be a struggle. You feel carried along by some invisible force, borne aloft on eagles' wings. Heaven reaches down and touches earth, and you're suspended between the two. Exertion becomes ecstasy. It's the "runner's high."

How does this happen? Many attribute it to a spike in dopamine and the release of endorphins that flood the body during exercise. These chemicals trigger a positive feeling in the body, similar to that caused by morphine. So is the runner's high chemical or divine? Does it matter? Is there a difference?

In his seminal book on depression, *The Noonday Demon*, Andrew Solomon writes: "Everything about a person is just chemical if one wants to think in those terms. ... The sun shines brightly and that's just chemical too, and it's chemical that rocks are hard, and that the sea is salt, and that certain springtime afternoons carry in their gentle breezes a quality of nostalgia that stirs the heart to longings and imaginings kept dormant by the snows of a long winter."

God, in his infinite wisdom and creativity, designed the mind, the body, and the chemical interactions between them. Solomon quotes Maggie Robinson, who argues: "You can say it's 'just chemistry.' I say there's nothing 'just' about chemistry." Indeed, how else does God communicate with humans but through physical matter? When we feel the runner's high, it can be both a chemical occurrence and the kiss of God. The two are inseparable.

For Christians, this inseparability is most clearly revealed in the Incarnation. When the Son of God took on human flesh, the physical and the divine bonded forever. Heaven kissed earth, and salvation broke forth upon the world. Indescribable joy became a possibility for human beings. This brush with joy happens whenever we truly encounter God. Sometimes that encounter happens during a run.

Experienced runners also know that the runner's high won't happen on every run. Like joy itself, the runner's high is mysterious and slippery. It's not a synthetic drug that you can manufacture. You can increase your likelihood of experiencing it, however, by running consistently. And when it does happen, it's a gift from God.

Saint Thomas Aquinas teaches that grace does not destroy nature, but perfects it. We get a little taste of this reality when we experience the runner's high. Powerful as the runner's high is, though, we shouldn't seek this experience like a drug fiend. (There's a reason running enthusiasts are sometimes called "run junkies.") As Catholic runners, we aren't addicts looking for a "hit." We run for other reasons: to get in shape, to maintain our fitness, or to be healthy for our loved ones. When we do feel the runner's high, though, we can enjoy it as the perfect gift from God that it is.

You likely won't experience that high every time you hit the road, but every now and then it happens — and you'll find yourself caught between heaven and earth.

PRAY
Thank you, Lord, for allowing me to taste the glorious gift of your joy when I run.

RUN
Next time you experience the runner's high, thank God for the gift. If you don't experience it today, keep running anyway, knowing that running is its own reward.

14

God Is a Runner, Too

But while he was yet at a distance, his father
saw him and had compassion, and ran
and embraced him and kissed him.

Luke 15:20

REFLECT

Stories about runners abound in the Bible. Some of these stories are deeply tragic. When King David's son was killed in battle, a messenger named Ahim´a-az ran to tell David the news (see 2 Sam 18:19–27). In the Garden of Gethsemane, a crowd armed with swords and clubs came to capture Jesus; in the melee, they grabbed one of his followers by his linen garment, and the young man ran away naked (see Mk 14:51).

Yet many of the stories of running in Scripture are filled with joy. Just a few days after Jesus' arrest, John outran Peter in his rush to see the empty tomb (see Jn 20:4). And my favorite runner in the Bible is the prodigal son's father. In Jesus' parable (see Lk 15:11–32), the lost son has squandered his inheritance, hit rock bottom, and decided to return home. He has rehearsed his apology and probably expects to be greeted by his father's wrath. Instead, when the father spots his son far in the distance, he runs to meet him and embraces him.

What an image. The father could (rightfully) have sat back and waited for his son to arrive, making him grovel for forgiveness. He could have sent servants to tell his son to turn around and never come back. But the father's heart is too full of love for that. Not only does he welcome his son back happily, he literally runs out to embrace him. Jesus told his disciples this parable because this is how God relates to us.

When we reject God, fall away, or sin, we feel tempted to avoid God. We assume he's angry with us. Nothing could be further from the truth. Not only is he waiting for us to return to him, he runs to meet us on our way. He himself closes the distance between him and us.

Anyone can return to God at any time. For Catholics, this happens uniquely in the Sacrament of Reconciliation. The Church has graciously provided a means for us to reconcile with our Father by confessing our sins and receiving absolution. "If we acknowledge our sins, he is faithful and just, and will forgive our sins and cleanse us from all unrighteousness" (1 Jn 1:9).

Some wonder why we can't just confess our sins privately and directly to God. In fact, we can and we should. But when we confess out loud to a priest in sacramental confession, a number of things happen. First, we open ourselves to receive the graces God imparts through the sacrament. Second, we acknowledge that our sin does not affect us alone: every sin we commit also impacts the community. The priest, as a representative of Christ and the Christian community, can then offer us absolution. Finally, there is something immensely healing about hearing out loud that we have been forgiven. The priest tells us: "Through the ministry of the Church may God give you pardon and peace, and I absolve you from your sins in the name of the Father, and of the Son, and of the Holy Spirit." Are there any more beautiful and freeing words than these? Confession to a priest is medicine for the mind and soul.

It's easy to think that going to confession is all about making us holy and more virtuous, and this is a big part of it. But according to the Church, the primary purpose of the sacrament is to heal us and restore us to right relationship with God. God wants us to be well. As Pope Francis said, confession is not a torture chamber, but the place we go to receive God's mercy. When we run to confession, we find God already waiting for us there. Pope Francis puts it beautifully: "We stand before a God who knows our sins, our betrayals, our denials, our wretchedness. And yet he is there waiting for us, ready to give himself completely to us, to lift us up."

So if you've sinned and need to confess, go as soon as you can. Don't walk. Run. Like John outrunning Peter to the empty tomb, God has beat you there. Because God is a runner, too, and he runs to you and to me.

PRAY
Father, thank you for the healing Sacrament of Reconciliation. Thank you for loving me and running to meet me. May I always run to meet you, too.

RUN
Thank God for the gift of confession (and if it's been a while since your last confession, find a church and go). After receiving absolution and doing the penance prescribed by the priest, offer up your next run in gratitude for God's forgiveness.

15

How Beautiful Are the Feet

How beautiful upon the mountains are the feet of him who brings good tidings, / who publishes peace, who brings good tidings of good, / who publishes salvation, who says to Zion, "Your God reigns."

Isaiah 52:7

REFLECT

Most people probably wouldn't describe feet as beautiful. Let's be real — they're kind of weird looking, and they're sometimes smelly. Feet are functional, yes. But beautiful? Well, the prophet Isaiah thought they were! Why? Because feet can bear God's message to the world.

For Catholics, running can be more than a fun, healthy

physical activity; it can be a witness to our faith. The act of maintaining our health shows others that we care about the body God gave us. Keeping ourselves fit, we are stronger and more capable of doing the work of God in our lives. But running provides an opportunity to witness in other practical ways, too.

Meeting runners with different worldviews gives us a natural opportunity to share our faith. Some people instinctively love running but have never thought of it in terms of a Creator who made them to love it. Through a mutual love of running, Christians can share our perspective with others. We don't have to smash them over the head with a Bible. We can just run alongside them. Who knows? Maybe people will see something in us they never considered before. Maybe hearts and minds can be opened, thanks to our feet propelling us forward to deliver God's message.

Consider starting a local running club that prays together during runs. Raise money for a local charity by recruiting sponsors for a race in your community. Bond with others who have different beliefs through your mutual love of the sport. It's a gentle, inoffensive way to connect on a natural level and share your faith. Like the herald bounding up the mountains in Isaiah, let your feet bear the Good News. Your options for employing running as a witness are limited only by your imagination and creativity.

I've met people from Christian running organizations like

Run For God (runforgod.com) at several races. Some Catholic dioceses organize running clubs to help their members stay fit, physically and spiritually. Whether racing for the sheer joy of it or using their running time to pray the Rosary as an "in-motion devotion," these people are synthesizing their running and their faith in fun, powerful ways.

In the 1980s, long-distance runner Alberto Salazar was, by his own admission, a nominal Catholic. If a twenty-mile training run conflicted with Mass on a Sunday, the run would always take priority. He accomplished great running feats, winning both the New York and Boston marathons. Eventually, however, a series of injuries sidelined him. Twelve years later, Salazar reconnected with his faith and took on one last race, a 53.75-mile ultramarathon in South Africa in 1994.

After almost quitting at the 30-mile point, Salazar regained his strength and started praying the Rosary out loud. "The crowd saw that I was humbled and could actually see there was a higher force working within me," Salazar shared. Many spectators began to cheer and pray the Rosary along with him. He finished the race.

Feet become beautiful when they take on the role of giving God glory. When they're enlisted to carry the Good News, they become elevated from the (literal) lowest part of the body to something grander. It's the mission that makes the feet beautiful.

Quoting Isaiah, Saint Paul said: "And how can men preach

unless they are sent? As it is written, 'How beautiful are the feet of those who preach good news!'" (Rom 10:15). Whether you're an elite ultramarathoner or you are training for a local 5K, your running and your faith can complement each other and shine a light that points others to God.

PRAY
Lord, let my feet be beautiful bearers of the Good News of your love for everyone.

RUN
During your training for an upcoming race, make an effort to befriend and share your faith with other runners. If you enjoy running with others, look into joining a local running club that will allow you to make new friends and share your faith as you run together.

16
Run in the Night

Even the darkness is not dark to you, the night is bright as day; for darkness is as light with you.
                                            Psalm 139:12

REFLECT

One of my favorite places to run is the 3.2-mile paved loop around the Rose Bowl Stadium in Pasadena, California. Throughout the day, it's filled with runners, cyclists, and dog walkers. When the sun goes down, it's lit up all night by street lamps every fifty yards or so, so you can run on it at any time you want. Generally, I prefer to run in the morning or early evening while it's light outside. But sometimes I can only fit in a run before the sun has come up or after it has gone down.

I recently went for a predawn run around the stadium loop. Even though the sky was pitch black, recreational joggers and walkers were already out on the course under the orange glow of the lights. By the time I completed the loop, the sun had begun to emerge, streaking the sky a fiery pink and scarlet, heralding a bright new morning. A magnificent sunrise is a great reward for a run in the dark.

Another of my favorite places to run is an unlit one-mile paved loop in a park outside my hometown in Kentucky. One morning, I drove there for a predawn run. Realizing as I exited the car that I'd forgotten my headlamp, I decided to try to run anyway. I had to run slowly and carefully in order not to veer off the course into bushes or a tree. When I reached a spot that cut through a wooded area, it grew even darker. My imagination kicked into anxious overdrive as I proceeded in the blackness. What was around me? Mountain lions? Snakes? Bandits? I couldn't see anything but the ground in front of my feet.

A Scripture verse came to mind: "Even the darkness is not dark to you, / the night is bright as day; / for darkness is as light with you" (Ps 139:12). Out there running in the pitch black, I couldn't see anything. But God could. To God, that early morning darkness was as bright as day. He could see everything around me as if it were noonday. The thought gave me comfort.

Still, running in the absolute dark like that was not a good idea. If you're going to run in the dark, always take precautions

— safety is paramount. Especially in the city and on roads, wear bright clothing and reflective gear so that drivers can see you. And don't listen to music through earphones, since you need to be extra alert and aware of your surroundings. (Many race organizers forbid participants from wearing earphones for this reason.)

Once you've prioritized your safety, you can enjoy the unique experience of running in the dark. Everything becomes enhanced. It's just you and the night, the sound of your breathing, and the noises around you, whether it's crickets or car horns. The setting is ideal for practicing mindfulness and being present in the moment. And it's a great time for attending to God.

A friend once told me about her experience running a distance relay race at night. Wearing a reflective vest, she carried a flashlight to illuminate the rural road in front of her. She could see only a few feet directly in front of her, while everything else was engulfed in black, yet it was enough light for her run. "It's the same way with life sometimes," she told me. Though we *want* to see the big picture, a few feet in front of us is all we *need* to see in order to keep moving forward. God gives us just enough light for our immediate needs. Psalm 119:105 puts it this way: "Your word is a lamp to my feet, / and a light to my path."

So the next time you go for a run in the darkness, remember: First, always be safe and alert. Then enter into the experience, enjoy it, and look for what God may be showing you in the peaceful hush of the dark.

PRAY
Light of the World, help me always to look to you for strength and guidance.

RUN
Invest in some reflective gear so you can run safely in the dark, and go for a run before dawn or after dusk. (Of course, make sure you're in a safe area, and bring along a cell phone.)

17
Run as Thanksgiving

Thanks be to God for his inexpressible gift!
2 Corinthians 9:15

REFLECT
Some days, I just don't feel like going for a run. We've all felt it. We're not inspired or motivated. We're tired or just plain lazy. But then I think about a friend of mine who used to be strong and physically active. He loved working out. Then one day, while trimming branches, he fell out of a tree and shattered his body. Today, he's confined to a bed, unable to move without assistance.

When I think about him and so many others — like accident victims and military veterans — who have suffered catastrophic injuries, I am struck by how fortunate I am to be able to move at all. Before I go for a run, I always say a prayer of thanksgiving that I'm physically able to do it. I offer up my run as a prayer of thanks to God for blessing me with legs, lungs, and mobility.

Often, we don't realize how blessed we are until we lose something we took for granted. My father, who has been a runner all his life, recently told me that his doctor suggested he may have to give up running because of lower back pain; the continual impact on his spine may be too much. My dad said he'll take up lower impact exercises like cycling and swimming to stay in shape, but it's hard. Any devoted runner knows that it's a great loss to have to give up the sport. There's nothing quite like running.

For most of us, the day will come when we can no longer do some activity we love. It might be playing basketball, painting, or playing an instrument, or it might be running. This awareness should be enough to make us grateful for what we can still do, and it should compel us to get out and do it while we can.

One way runners give thanks is by using the gift of physical health and strength that God has given us — by getting out and running. This practice of thanksgiving can, in turn, condition us to be grateful in all areas of our lives — to give thanks to our family members, coworkers, and parish servants for the work they do and the sacrifices they make. Gratitude begets gratitude. The more we run and the more we give thanks, the better runners and the better people we will become.

Most people possess a sense of gratitude. It doesn't matter if they're religious or agnostic, people of faith or people with no belief in a higher power. At some point, in some way, for some thing, we are all grateful. Gratitude implies someone to be grateful to. Some thank something nebulous like "the universe" or their "lucky stars." As Christians, we direct our gratitude to our God, who is not a distant deity but a Person. When we encounter him and his deep love for us, our life is never the same.

One way to thank someone for a gift is to give them something in return. On my best days, I turn my run into a physical prayer of thanksgiving that I give to the God who has given me everything. With each forward step, I pray with Saint Paul: "Thanks be to God for his inexpressible gift!"

PRAY
Father God, let me always give you thanks with my body and my soul.

RUN
Consciously offer up your run today as a prayer of thanksgiving for being able to move.

18

Run as Intercession

*Pray at all times in the Spirit, with all prayer
and supplication. To that end keep alert with all
perseverance, making supplication for all the saints.*
Ephesians 6:18

REFLECT

All baptized Christians are called to pray and intercede for others before God. One of the beautiful aspects of Christianity is that there's no one right way to do this. We can be creative. We can pray with our mind, and we can pray with our body. We can pray on our knees, and we can pray on a racetrack. If the whole world is God's, then even a running trail can be the throne room in which we bring to him the needs of others.

How do we do this? It doesn't mean constantly walking around with our heads bowed, eyes closed, and hands clasped. It's more of an attitude, a disposition toward open communication with God. Offering up our run as intercession for others is a great way to "pray constantly" (1 Thes 5:17).

Sometimes this can be mentally taxing, as it's hard to remember who needs our prayers or what exactly we should be asking for them. Maybe we don't know exactly who or what to pray for, but God knows. Jesus assures us that "your Father knows what you need before you ask him" (Mt 6:8). So entrust your run to God as a prayer for others, offering up your exertion and trusting in his perfect knowledge and wisdom to meet the needs of others.

We think about many different things when we run, and sometimes people pop into our thoughts. As people cross my mind when I run, I lift them up to God. I pray for their health and well-being and that God will meet whatever specific need they have. Since I don't always know what their needs are, sometimes I simply lift up their names to God. For instance, if my friend Mike crosses my mind, I just pray "Jesus: Mike." And I leave the rest to Jesus.

Saint Paul tells us that we can trust that the Holy Spirit knows exactly what to pray for: "Likewise the Spirit helps us in our weakness; for we do not know how to pray as we ought, but the Spirit himself intercedes for us with sighs too deep for words.

And he who searches the hearts of men knows what is the mind of the Spirit, because the Spirit intercedes for the saints according to the will of God" (Rom 8:26–27).

The seventeenth-century Carmelite mystic Brother Lawrence talked of carrying on a "habitual, silent, and secret conversation with God." He wrote: "The time of business does not differ with me from the time of prayer; and in the noise and clatter of my kitchen, while several persons are at the same time calling for different things, I possess God in as great tranquility as if I were on my knees."

In the same way, when we offer our run as intercession, we can say: "Jesus, here's my run, here's my effort … use it to meet the needs of all the people you give me to pray for." We are all intercessors. Turn your runs into prayers for others' needs.

PRAY
Heavenly Father, today I lift up my run as a prayer for all those in need who cross my mind.

RUN
Offer up your run today as intercession for someone in your life who needs prayers.

19

Run as Service

*Truly, I say to you, as you did it to one of the
least of these my brethren, you did it to me.*
Matthew 25:40

REFLECT
What if you could improve your fitness and help change lives at the same time? Numerous charities sponsor races. When you register for one of these races, your money goes toward raising awareness of and furthering their mission.

Near my hometown in Kentucky, there's a restaurant called DV8 Kitchen. It employs people in the early stages of substance abuse recovery. Often, these people have trouble finding work while they're trying to get their lives back on track. According to the company's website, "DV8 Kitchen was developed and operates as a second chance employment opportunity for people who are trying to redirect their lives." Each year, the restaurant sponsors the DV8K Life Changing Run, the proceeds of which go toward hiring second chance employees. This year's race proceeds went toward buying a delivery van for their wholesale bakery.

Another annual race in Kentucky is the CASA (Court Appointed Special Advocates) Superhero 5K. Race participants dress up in superhero costumes and raise money to support abused children. It's fun, and it serves a good cause.

Do an online search for races in your area. You are sure to find one that contributes to a charity or business that serves those in need. It could be a fundraiser for a Catholic school, a homeless shelter, or the American Red Cross. There are countless causes in need of support, and you as a runner have the ability to contribute toward any of them. What cause does your heart respond to? Find a race that supports it, and sign up. You get to practice running and serve at the same time. It's another way to be a practical witness by your running.

Jesus told this story about his eventual return:

> Then the King will say to those at his right hand, "Come, O blessed of my Father, inherit the kingdom prepared for you from the foun-

dation of the world; for I was hungry and you gave me food, I was thirsty and you gave me drink, I was a stranger and you welcomed me, I was naked and you clothed me, I was sick and you visited me, I was in prison and you came to me."

Then the righteous will answer him, "Lord, when did we see you hungry and feed you, or thirsty and give you drink? And when did we see you a stranger and welcome you, or naked and clothe you? And when did we see you sick or in prison and visit you?" And the King will answer them, "Truly, I say to you, as you did it to one of the least of these my brethren, you did it to me" (Mt 25:34–40).

In the same spirit, why not benefit your own body and serve Christ in others at the same time?

PRAY
Jesus, let me serve you in others by running.

RUN
Train for a local race that supports a cause you believe in, knowing that you're serving God and others as you prepare. Have fun and serve at the same time!

20
Run to Heal

He heals the brokenhearted, and binds up their wounds.
                                                    Psalm 147:3

REFLECT

It is well known that running has the power to improve our cardiovascular health and immune system and to fight disease. But the benefits of running go beyond the physical. Running can also help heal our hearts and minds. I experienced this after my marriage collapsed.

My former wife and I used to run together. We'd train on trails and neighborhood streets, and we competed together in several races. It was a good bonding activity, and it kept us healthy. When my marriage fell apart and I moved out to live on my own for the first time in six years, I was devastated. I cried a lot. I slept late into the day. For a while, I drank too much. But I knew that this kind of self-destructive grieving was not sustainable. I eventually cut back on the Miller Lite six-packs and started dragging myself out of bed at a normal hour.

Thankfully, running was an ingrained habit for me by then. So despite my pain, I still hit the road for a run every other day or so. Along with time, my faith, and emotional support from friends and family, the practice of running was a crucial factor in my healing from the trauma of divorce.

Running three to five miles gave my mind a break from running over my situation. My head filled with other thoughts, which dissipated my feelings of sadness, failure, and regret. When I did ruminate on my ruined relationship during a run, I found myself able to think more constructive thoughts. What had gone wrong? How could I do better in the future? With each forward step, a growing sense of hope wiped out negative thoughts and feelings. Running for an hour was a great coping mechanism. It beat staring at the TV, drinking too much, and sleeping in.

A few months after my ex and I separated, I started training for the Pasadena Half Marathon. Having a goal on the calendar forced me to get out and exercise. Within a few weeks, I was doing ten-mile workouts in preparation for the race. These long runs both boosted my mood and gave me time to pray. I asked God for strength to get through the divorce. I prayed for my ex, that God would care for her and bring us both through this sad experience stronger and happier. Sometimes I cleared my head of any thoughts at all and simply enjoyed God's presence.

Finishing the half marathon gave me a positive feeling of accomplishment. It reminded me that humans are capable of more than we think and that I was going to survive the divorce. It would take several more years, but I gradually found myself feeling better and becoming productive again. Running was a huge part of that process.

Running is also a fantastic stress reliever. It increases levels of neurotransmitters like serotonin and norepinephrine, which heighten our sense of calm and well-being. Running on a treadmill works well, but running outside may be even more beneficial.

For generations, health practitioners have extolled the benefits of getting out in the sunlight, walking among trees, and gazing at plants and flowers. There's something about being in nature that renews the body and mind. Japanese tradition calls the restorative practice of immersing yourself in nature *shinrin-yoku* ("forest bathing"). Traditional Native American cultures have long promoted living in harmony with nature. Whatever you call it, there's an unmistakable connection between being in nature and our emotional and physical well-being. When you can, consider running on woodland trails or other courses outside urban areas.

Surviving any kind of emotional trauma takes prayer and support. Sometimes it takes counseling. But sometimes it also takes a pair of running shoes. Scripture tells us that God "heals the broken-hearted, / and binds up their wounds" (Ps 147:3). For me, one of the ways he did this was through running. Perhaps he wants to work a similar healing in you. Ask God to turn your runs into a time of restoration, in whatever way you most need.

PRAY
Dear God, thank you for the healing power of running. Help me take advantage of this amazing gift.

RUN
Try running outdoors today, in a city park or on a wooded trail. As you run, soak in and enjoy the connection with nature.

21

The Gift of Encouragement

*Therefore encourage one another and build
one another up, just as you are doing.*

1 Thessalonians 5:11

REFLECT

The most vital people in a race are not always the runners. Sometimes they are the ones along the side of the course who have come to cheer the runners on. Just as good nutrition helps our bodies keep going, encouragement can lift our spirits right when we need it.

In races where I was dragging along, pushing through the pain, I've suddenly heard my name: "Great job, Chris!" Sometimes the person shouting is a complete stranger who sees my name on my bib. Even when the bib displays only your entry number, people shout anyway: "You got this!" "Great job!" "You're almost there!" During one race, a row of children waited on the sideline, stretching out their little hands to give me high fives as I breezed past them. It may seem like a small thing, but it's not. All of us need encouragement to keep going and to stay motivated.

During times when we can't race — maybe we're recovering from an injury, or we didn't have sufficient time to train — we can still participate by joining other observers along the course and offering encouragement to the racers. One great way to do this is by making a colorful sign displaying an inspiring quote, a motivational message, or a funny saying and holding it up for passing runners to see. Your sign may be just what they need to propel them on to the finish line.

Encouragement doesn't have to be restricted to races, either. See someone jogging down your neighborhood street? Give them a fist pump or a thumbs up. Acknowledge the effort they're making to improve themselves. The gift of encouragement is one we sometimes need to receive, but it's also one we get to give.

Do you know someone who is going through a hard time? Perhaps they are struggling emotionally or financially or grieving the loss of a loved one. Maybe they're suffering through infidelity or divorce or struggling with addiction. Or they're just lonely. They might be discouraged by their children's behavior or simply feeling that their life doesn't hold much meaning. Give them a call. Write an uplifting letter. Pay them a visit. Share some comforting words. Or just sit with them if that's what they need. Sometimes simply knowing that someone else is thinking about us, praying for us, and rooting for us is enough. There are countless ways to be an encouragement to others, and it can make all the difference.

We all need help along the way. Crossing the finish line is a great feeling, but it can feel just as good to help someone else do it. So don't be afraid to encourage others, both in their running and in life; you never know how God might use you.

PRAY
Lord, help me always to encourage the people around me.

RUN
Go online and find a race that will take place in your area (most likely on a Saturday morning). Pick a spot along the course, and cheer on the runners as they pass by.

22
Run with the Rain

Therefore, since we are surrounded by so great a cloud of witnesses, let us also lay aside every weight, and sin which clings so closely, and let us run with perseverance the race that is set before us.

Hebrews 12:1

REFLECT

It never rains in Southern California — or so they say.

As I pulled my car into the parking lot around five-thirty in the morning, a light drizzle began to coat the windshield. It was the morning of the Huntington Beach Half Marathon, the first time I'd ever attempt running 13.1 miles. For the previous three months, I had trained under sunny blue skies at this same spot, a beachside strip of road that hugs the sparkling Pacific. But on this race day morning, it was unexpectedly gloomy and wet.

Walking through the chilly air to join the other runners near the starting corral, I felt hopeful that the sky might clear up soon as night dissolved into morning. But as the race announcer's voice boomed from the speakers, summoning us to the starting line, the drizzle built into a soft shower. By the time the gun cracked and we crossed the line, it was a torrential downpour.

I pressed on through the sheets of heavy water slashing sideways across my body. One mile, two miles … the rain didn't let up. Four miles, five miles … I hadn't planned for this, but I was doing okay. I was soggy but no longer shivering, thanks to my elevated body heat.

Then, around the halfway point of the course, I noticed something odd. The edges of the road were littered with discarded, sopping-wet clothes. Other runners were unzipping their hoodies, yanking off their sweaters, stripping away their sweatpants, and then tossing them aside. These runners didn't want their drenched apparel to negatively affect their finish times, so they were literally casting aside the things that weighed them down.

Dodging the occasional cast-off track jacket on the road, I realized something else: like it or not, sometimes the day is going to bring something we didn't plan for. You may have to run in conditions that aren't ideal. Instead of getting upset, you can choose to accept what's happening. Feel the beads of water streak your face. Let your hair get messed up. Stick out your tongue and taste the droplets. Drink from the heavens. After all, if there's anything you can't control, it's the weather. So why fight it?

Nearly two hours and fifteen minutes after starting my first half marathon, I approached the finish line. The deluge began to recede into a soft drizzle. My legs felt weary as a smiling volunteer slipped a finisher's medal around my neck. My hips ached as I shuffled to the snack table to grab a banana. I felt great. And the rain stopped.

We race finishers mingled under clearing skies, enjoying our shared accomplishment. I looked out over the gray ocean in the distance. If God "sends rain on the just and on the unjust" (Mt 5:45), we were a thousand soaked sinners that day, and it was glorious in its own way. So when the rain comes, don't run against it. Run with it.

PRAY
God of the heavens, help me be present and see your goodness in every circumstance.

RUN
Whether you're running in heat, rain, or snow today, practice being present in the conditions God has given you. Next time it rains, plan to go for a quick run so you, too, can experience the joy of running with the rain.

23

Far More than All We Ask or Think

Now to him who by the power at work within us is able to do far more abundantly than all that we ask or think, to him be glory in the Church and in Christ Jesus to all generations, for ever and ever. Amen.

Ephesians 3:20–21

REFLECT

It was a perfect day for the City to the Sea Half Marathon in San Luis Obispo, California. The sky was deep blue, the sun was out, and a light breeze blew in off the ocean, making the temperature ideal for a 13.1-mile race. I wasn't trying to beat any records that day. I had trained adequately, and I just wanted to enjoy the scenery and the run. But there was a surprise in store.

The race started in the quaint city center, then funneled onto a narrow rural road that cut through rolling, green farmland. Curious cows watched as runners bounded past. I had found a nice pace, and the run was going well. Eventually, I passed the eight-mile marker on the side of the road. Only five left to go. I pressed on.

A few minutes later, I saw the next mile marker in the distance. It read "Mile 8." Wait ... hadn't I just passed the eight-mile point? As I got closer to the marker, I could make it out more clearly. Yep, it definitely said "Mile 8." Had I been hallucinating a mile back? Was my mind playing tricks on me? Had I accidentally run through a time warp that swallowed up the last mile into some mysterious vortex? I was confused, but all I could do was keep going. The next mile marker read "Mile 9." Okay, we were back on track.

The country road opened up into a neighborhood, and I climbed a hill past a stretch of brick houses with well-manicured lawns. Finally, I heard the distant din of music and celebration up ahead: the finish line. Feeling a little more spent than I'd anticipated, I crossed the finish line and checked my time. I had completed the race in about two hours and forty-five minutes, fifteen minutes longer than I had timed for myself.

I never talked with the race organizers, but I'm convinced I

Far More than All We Ask or Think 103

wasn't hallucinating when I passed the eight-mile marker twice. Somehow, someone had misjudged the distance and set up two eight-mile markers. I had actually run 14.1 miles. The extra fifteen minutes tacked on to my finish time convinced me. It was odd, but it taught me something: we are capable of more than we think.

If someone had told me before the race that I was going to have to run an extra mile, I might not have been mentally prepared. But I didn't know, so I was able to do it anyway. Of course, I couldn't have done it at all if I hadn't been building up my endurance in the weeks leading up to the race. I had prepared and, consequently, I was able to go even farther than I'd imagined.

This incident reminded me of something I experienced a few years earlier on a mission trip in Kenya. At the hotel in Nairobi, I decided to get in a quick strength workout. I stacked the weights on the barbell: 35 pounds on each side, so I'd be bench pressing 70 pounds. But when I heaved the barbell off the rack, I could barely lift it. I was used to lifting this amount, so why was I struggling so mightily? I didn't know. I pumped out a few more wobbly reps, then racked the weights.

Only later did I realize that the Kenyan gym numbered its weights by kilograms instead of pounds. What I thought was 35 pounds was actually 35 kilos, which equaled 77 pounds. I had been lifting 154 pounds — more than twice the weight I thought! No wonder I could only manage a few reps. Still, I did them. But if I had known I was going to have to lift double the weight I normally do, I doubt I could have managed one rep. My mind would have gotten in the way.

What's the lesson? If we build our endurance and rely on God for help, we are sometimes able to do more than we thought possible. I don't recommend attempting to lift twice what you're used to or running fourteen miles when you only trained for thirteen. But the mind and the body are amazing, and sometimes the race we plan for ends up being longer than we expected. When those times come, God will give us the strength to endure. With God, anything is possible.

PRAY
Dear God, "provide [us] with every blessing in abundance, so that [we] may always have enough of everything and may provide in abundance for every good work" (2 Cor 9:8).

RUN
Try adding an extra five minutes or quarter mile to your run today to increase your endurance. Remember, you can do more than you think. If you are preparing for a race, bear this in mind as your event gets closer.

24

Run for Fun

Rejoice in the Lord always; again I will say, Rejoice.
                                              Philippians 4:4

REFLECT

Their bulging black eyes sized me up. They snorted through flat noses, and their tongues flopped out. They were here to participate in the annual Great Pug Run 5K, an event held every year to raise awareness and support for the Bluegrass Pug Rescue of Kentucky. I had signed up to race alongside the pugs. Why? Because I adore pugs. Also, because I figured they were the only competition I had a real shot at beating in a race.

The event kicked off with a forty-yard pug dash. Owners lined up their dogs at the starting line. The announcer shouted: "Ready, set … go!" The pugs exploded onto the course like a set of pool balls, flying in all directions. Some darted toward the finish line. Others chased each other back and forth across the course. Another stopped to pee on some dandelions. Turns out they didn't care too much about winning a race — they just wanted to have fun. A few minutes after the comic debacle of the forty-yard dash, human runners gathered to start the 5K. The course was a hilly grass-and-dirt trail through a park bordering horse farms.

We run for many reasons: To get in shape. To stay healthy. To challenge ourselves. But honestly, I can't think of many better reasons to run than helping sick and abandoned puppies. Not everything is a competition. Sometimes it's enough to simply celebrate the good things in life, like joyous, smush-faced little dogs.

We can learn a lot about joy from the pugs at that race. They were not concerned with proving themselves. They weren't at the race to win anything. On the day of the Great Pug Run, humans were encouraged to party with their pugs, entering into their pure spirit of carefree abandon. There were many amusing sights along the course. Some pugs waddled on their leashes in front of their owners. Others were strapped to their owners' backs in a harness. Some hitched a ride in a stroller pushed by their people. Some pugs simply called it quits a quarter mile into the race, and their humans had to pick them up and carry them across the finish line. (Pugs are not known for their endurance.) Their athletic prowess was about equal to mine. In fact, a few pugs pulled ahead and beat me. Others just watched, curly tails wagging, as I ran past them. At the end of the race, they were all happy to jump on me and be cuddled and petted.

Saint Padre Pio said: "Serve the Lord with laughter." Saint John Bosco, famous for his joy, performed magic tricks, juggled, walked the tightrope, and opened a carnival show as part of his ministry. Hardly a sour-faced saint, Bosco advised: "Enjoy yourself as much as you like — if only you keep from sin." Flannery O'Connor noted: "Only if we are secure in our beliefs can we see the comical side of the universe." And the mirthful Catholic philosopher G. K. Chesterton observed: "It is the test of a good religion whether you can joke about it."

So racing with the pugs that day, I chose not to worry about my finish time or impressing anyone, including myself. Instead, I enjoyed the funny-looking dogs and their antic behavior. I took a lesson from their lack of guile, and I tried to be present in the moment the way they were.

There's a broader lesson here for all of us. The Christian life doesn't have to be glum. Saint Paul urges us: "Rejoice in the Lord always." And then for emphasis, he adds: "Again I will say, Rejoice." Despite the many trials and sufferings we experience, life in Christ is meant to be lived with joy. Sometimes all it takes to remind us of this truth is a fun run — with pugs, if you can manage it!

PRAY
Lord, let me always remember — and practice — the joy of living in you.

RUN
On your run today, forget striving for times and distances. Just be present and have fun.

25
Alien Race

*Set your minds on things that are above,
not on things that are on earth.*

Colossians 3:2

REFLECT

In the middle of the Nevada desert exists a mysterious place known as Area 51. It's officially a highly classified US Air Force training range, but conspiracy theories and legends have sprung up around it. Many think Area 51 houses artifacts of aliens and UFOs. It lies along Nevada State Route 375, also known as the Extraterrestrial Highway.

When I learned about the annual Extraterrestrial Full Moon Midnight Half Marathon held nearby, I decided to check it out. I figured it would be a cool experience to run through the Southwestern desert under a full moon. Maybe I'd even catch sight of a runaway Martian. Either way, it would beat running on a treadmill in the gym for two hours.

When I arrived around midnight in the dusty, remote parking lot 150 miles north of the Las Vegas Strip, it was packed with runners draped in glow-in-the-dark wristbands and necklaces. Some people were painted green. Others were dressed in bulky spaceman costumes. I stretched and mingled with a few alien enthusiasts. Then the race started, and the motley band of runners launched across the line.

The first stretch of the course was uphill, but thankfully it was dark so I couldn't see how steep the incline was. I struggled forward, the road illuminated only by pale moonlight and the small lamp strapped to my forehead. After the first couple of miles, the pack thinned out and I found myself running alone, accompanied only by the sound of my breathing and the occasional moan of an unseen cow somewhere in the fields on either side of the road.

At one point, I had to veer off the road to relieve myself. The race organizers had warned us to be careful that we didn't step on a rattlesnake, so I watched my step. Resuming my run in the hushed dark, I had plenty of time to think.

I've often thought that if proof of extraterrestrial life were discovered, it would be pretty amazing. It wouldn't negate the existence of God or anything in the Bible. It would only broaden our

Alien Race 111

understanding of what exists in the vast universe God created. Far from disproving God, it would prove he's bigger than we could ever imagine. I thought of a line from *Hamlet*: "There are more things in heaven and earth, Horatio, / Than are dreamt of in your philosophy."

The perennial fascination with the possibility that intelligent life exists beyond our planet just points to the fact that inside each of us is a desire to know we're not alone in the universe. It's a sign of our longing for heaven. As C. S. Lewis observed: "If we find ourselves with a desire that nothing in this world can satisfy, the most probable explanation is that we were made for another world." Maybe that's one reason why we were all racing through the night dressed like aliens.

Do you ever feel alone in the cosmos? You're not. The Nicene Creed proclaims: "I believe in one God, the Father almighty, maker of heaven and earth, of all things visible and invisible." The same God who formed a billion stars formed you. Stars shine. Galaxies swirl. And you run. And when you do, you participate in the great cosmic celebration of all creation.

After a couple of hours, the extraterrestrial race ended at a small diner called the Little A'Le'Inn. Kitschy pictures of aliens, meteor craters, and spaceships plastered the walls. I sat down to enjoy the pancakes, bacon, and eggs that awaited the course finishers. I didn't encounter any flying saucers or little green men on that run, but I did see some strange sights. And I was reminded how glorious God's world is — here on Earth and beyond. As an old hymn proclaims: "This is my Father's world/And to my listening ears/All nature sings, and round me rings/The music of the spheres."

I smiled as a thought occurred. If spindly white aliens with massive eyes were to visit our planet, they'd probably think we humans look pretty strange, too. They might even wonder: Why do these odd beings run through the desert in the middle of the night dressed like us?

After our two-thirty-in-the-morning breakfast, busses shuttled the runners back to our vehicles. On the ride back, I chatted with my fellow racing pilgrims. We were all just strangers in a strange land who suspected, whether we knew it or not, that there was something bigger out there than all of us.

PRAY
God of the heavens, thank you for creating me as part of your vast, wonderful universe.

RUN
On your run today, meditate on the awesome reality that, along with all the stars and planets and life in the universe, you are God's glorious creation.

26
Race Preparation

Every athlete exercises self-control in all things. They do it to receive a perishable wreath, but we an imperishable.
                                           1 Corinthians 9:25

REFLECT
I willingly signed up to run 26.2 miles. What was I thinking? Many people would only attempt to run such a distance if they were forced to do so — or maybe if somebody paid them. Instead, I paid money for the opportunity.

Maybe it's because I was thinking with my heart, not my brain. As Blaise Pascal said: "The heart has its reasons of which reason knows nothing." For many runners, completing a marathon is the ultimate rite of passage. Either way, I would be facing that daunting distance in just a few months.

I blame the Greeks. In 490 BC, a Greek herald named Pheidippides ran 25 miles from Marathon to Athens to announce the Greek victory over Persia at the Battle of Marathon. Legend has it that he breathlessly delivered the message "Joy, we win!" and then fell over dead. He died with the word *joy* on his tongue. Nearly 2,500 years later, in 1896, officials organizing the first modern Olympic Games named the long-distance race the "marathon" and set its distance at 40 kilometers (24.85 miles) to commemorate Pheidippides's sacrifice.

At the 1908 Olympic Games in London, Queen Alexandra of Britain requested that the race begin on the lawn of Windsor Castle so that the royal children could watch the start of the event. This added an extra mile or so to the distance, bringing the length of the marathon to 26.2 miles. It has remained that distance ever since.

Nobody can run even a 5K, let alone a marathon, without preparing. Pheidippides was a professional long-distance runner, so he had a lot of training under his belt. When I registered for my first marathon, the farthest I'd run was 13.1 miles, half the official marathon distance. So I would have to prepare.

Over the weeks, I gradually increased my mileage. Three miles. Five. Eight. Ten. My body acclimated. On weekdays after work, I ran as many miles as I had time for. I reserved weekends for longer runs, eventually working my way up to eighteen miles on Saturday or Sunday.

I also researched how to nourish myself properly. During runs longer than an hour, I strapped on a CamelBak containing seventy ounces of water so I'd have steady hydration. I also consumed energizing jelly beans or Clif nutrition bars to keep my glucose levels up. I took walk breaks when necessary to preserve my muscle strength and endurance.

As a safety precaution, I brought along my wallet. Who knew when I might have to stop at a convenience store along the route and buy a carb-filled sports drink? And if I got hit by a car or collapsed on the way, a Good Samaritan could find my ID and call for help.

I also brought my cell phone in case I ran out of steam and needed to call someone for a ride back home. Usually, I ran in a loop beginning and ending at my home, but one Sunday morning, I ran eighteen miles away from our apartment, then called my wife to come pick me up in the next town.

That's what it takes to prepare for a long race. Gradually build up your mileage and endurance. Have nutritional supplements handy to keep you fueled along the way. Take safety precautions so you're ready for emergencies. Throughout the long training process, your body and mind are being conditioned for the great race that's ahead. When the day of the big event arrives, you can be confident that you've done all you could to be ready.

It's the same with any challenge in life. You don't become a surgeon overnight; you go through years of training and education, so that when the crucial moment comes, you'll be ready to perform. A singer or musician trains tirelessly on her vocals or instrument in order to make beautiful sounds. In a relationship — marriage or other — you become a better lover by practicing love and self-sacrifice over time. By enduring life's many losses and challenges, you strengthen yourself and build up endurance to do better in the days ahead.

Whether you're preparing for a marathon or a shorter race, never try to launch out until you're ready. Preparation is key. This is true for a running race, and it's also true for life's trials and the race that leads to eternal life. As Saint Paul said, we "do not run aimlessly" (1 Cor 9:26). Always prepare!

PRAY

God, help me always to properly prepare for the races ahead, both physical and spiritual.

RUN

Today, revisit your race preparation plan. Have you been gradually building up your miles to increase your endurance? In your run today, think about adding on just a bit more — a quarter, a half, or even a full mile.

27

Phoenix Rising

I can do all things in him who strengthens me.
                                    Philippians 4:13

REFLECT

I suspect it was the spaghetti. I had come to Phoenix, Arizona, to run the annual Rock 'n' Roll Arizona Marathon, my first attempt to run 26.2 miles. The night before the race, I fueled up on carbs at an Italian restaurant and left feeling energized, ready for a good night's sleep.

But I awakened in the night feeling queasy. When the alarm clock went off, I stirred awake, tired and nauseated. However, I had a marathon to run. I had not trained for the past six months, logging countless hours and enduring knee aches and plantar fasciitis, for nothing. I couldn't give up now; I was going to tackle this race. I repeated Philippians 4:13 to myself: "I can do all things in him who strengthens me." I was about to put that Scripture to the test.

All I could manage for breakfast was a few bites of scrambled eggs and some oatmeal. At the starting line in downtown Phoenix, people stretched, jogged, and waited anxiously in the chilly January air. The atmosphere crackled with the mysterious live-wire energy that permeates the start of a competitive event. I liked the energy even though I wasn't feeling well.

Finally, a pistol cracked, and the race started. A mass of humanity, tens of thousands of people, surged forward in waves. I had devised a strategy: I would start with a brief walk, then pick up the pace. But after a half mile of slow jogging, acid reflux attacked and I felt my meager breakfast rising in my throat. So I slowed down and walked some more. I kept up this cycle for miles, until eventually I reached the midpoint of the race.

Here and there, wounded competitors littered the side of the course, receiving medical treatment for blisters and strains. At least I wasn't injured ... yet. I kept my eyes on the asphalt before me and pressed on until mile 18. That's when I hit the dreaded "wall," and that morning I could not push past it. I had to stop running. All I could manage was walking, and even that didn't look pretty. An elderly woman breezed past me. I glanced back to see if there was anyone left behind me. Yes, a good number of runners still straggled behind, offering me a small glimmer of encouragement. Maybe I wouldn't finish dead last.

I shuffled past a race volunteer with a bullhorn who shouted encouragement to the passing racers. "Go, number 544! You're doing great!" he bellowed. "That's it, number 723, looking good! You can do this!" But when I ran past the enthusiastic announcer, he fell silent. I don't blame him. I resembled a sweat-drenched zombie with wooden planks for legs. My face was scrunched in a grimace of pain. Still, I pressed on.

A marker came into view: "Mile 22." The next miles passed in a hot blur of sunlight and throbbing thighs. Then I heard it … the beautiful cacophony of music and chattering race finishers. The end was near. I picked up my pace and actually jogged the last quarter mile. The race took me six and a half hours. However I got there, I had now joined the ranks of marathon finishers.

The spiritual life is a marathon, too. No matter how well you prepare, there will be times when you get sick and weary and have to slow down to a walk. But that doesn't mean you quit the race. You keep moving forward as best you can. And just when you think you can't go on, you'll see the finish line in the distance. God gives you the strength to press on. Like me in Phoenix, you may cross the finish line feeling utterly depleted. But with God's help, you will finish. And, though exhausted and hobbling, you'll learn that all things are possible through him who strengthens you.

PRAY
Lord, thank you for enabling me to accomplish what I never thought possible.

RUN
Run today knowing that your training or upcoming race — whatever distance you have chosen — is not a sprint. Focus on gradually building up your endurance, slow and steady.

28
Personal Best

So we do not lose heart. Though our outer man is wasting away, our inner man is being renewed every day. For this slight momentary affliction is preparing for us an eternal weight of glory beyond all comparison, because we look not to the things that are seen but to the things that are unseen; for the things that are seen are transient, but the things that are unseen are eternal.
2 Corinthians 4:16–18

REFLECT
In running culture, there is a particular standard that every runner strives to achieve: personal best. A runner's personal best is their best time at a specific race distance.

I achieved my personal best one year at the Santa Barbara Wine Country Half Marathon in Solvang, California, a town modeled after an old-world Danish village, complete with Danish bakeries and windmill-topped hotels. I didn't set out to achieve my personal best that day. I was just going to run through the countryside, listen to my iPod, and enjoy the scenery.

I ran the first mile without music, choosing instead to soak in the ambient sounds — my own rhythmic breathing, chirping birds, chattering runners, and the thup-thup-thup of our shoes on the paved road. I quickly fell into a comfortable cadence and never did turn on my iPod.

At the midpoint of the course, the road zig-zagged all the way to the top of a looming, steep hill. From a distance, the runners criss-crossing the ascent resembled souls ascending the seven terraces of the mountain in Dante's *Purgatorio*.

I've never been a big fan of hills (or purgatory), so I assumed I might have to slow down and walk parts of this one. But when I started up the incline, I found myself feeling stronger than I thought, so I kept running. At the summit, volunteers handed out water at an aid station. The reward for conquering the hill was a breathtaking view of the Santa Ynez Valley, filled with rolling vineyards that stretched for miles in the distance. As I ticked off the miles, I picked out runners ahead of me as targets, planning with each one to stop for a short walk break once I reached them. But with each runner I passed, my energy never waned. So

I just kept on running.

It's a mystery why some days we feel like we can run nonstop, while other days each step is a brutal challenge. Maybe I had consumed just the right amount of carbohydrates and protein before the race. Maybe I had trained exceptionally well, building up my fitness and endurance. Whatever it was, I was firing on all cylinders that morning. A few times, I thought of checking the Nike fitness app on my iPod to see how far I'd run. But I decided against it, choosing to stay in the moment.

I came upon two guys walking and chatting about why in the world anyone willingly chooses to run such distances. "Are we just crazy?" one of the racers asked. Passing them, I thought I had the answer: it's for moments like this, when everything else falls away and you feel you could just keep going forever.

Approaching the final leg of the course, which returned us to the town center, I assumed I'd finish the race in a little over two hours, as with all my previous half marathons. Then I saw the digital race clock above the finish line in the distance. To my surprise, it read 1:58:30. I was shocked. I had been running faster than I thought, and I actually had a chance of coming in at under two hours.

I kicked my legs and lungs into high gear and sprinted toward the finish line, crossing it at around 1:59:25. A sub-two-hour half marathon finish time is no great feat for many runners, but it was for me — it was my personal best, and I felt amazing.

The profound sense of accomplishment we can get from achieving a personal record carries over into all areas of a runner's life. It reveals the strength we never knew we had. It shows us we are capable of accomplishing great things. It fills us with confidence and joy. Olympian Eric Liddell said that when he ran, he felt God's pleasure. I felt it that day, too, and thanked my Maker for the gift of running.

We can't be at our best every day. That's okay and natural. But we can always strive toward achieving our best. Some days we'll reach it, and some days we won't. When we do, we can celebrate. When we don't, we can know that the next personal best is always something to look forward to.

PRAY
Lord, help me strive to achieve my personal best, in running and in life.

RUN
Today on your run, go a little bit farther or a little bit longer than you did yesterday, knowing that you're always striving toward your personal best.

29

We Never Run Alone

Where shall I go from your Spirit? Or where shall I flee from your presence? / If I ascend to heaven, you are there! If I make my bed in Sheol, you are there! If I take the wings of the morning and dwell in the uttermost parts of the sea, / even there your hand shall lead me, and your right hand shall hold me.
                                                    Psalm 139: 7–10

REFLECT

Almost every time an angel appears to someone in the New Testament, it says the same words: "Do not be afraid." It's a reasonable exhortation — if most of us saw an actual angel, our first response would probably be abject fear. So the angels let people know right away that there's no reason to be scared, because God is bringing good news. And what's the good news? More often than not, whatever the specific circumstances, the good news is that God is present and active in their lives. We are not alone.

What does this have to do with running?

Some people like to run with a partner or in a group. It keeps them accountable, and they enjoy the communal aspect. Chatting with someone during a run makes the time go by faster. Partners can motivate one another to keep going (or to get started in the first place). If this is what works to get you moving, great. I prefer to run by myself. It's my personal time to clear my head, gather my thoughts, brainstorm ideas for work, listen to music, and pray. I also enjoy running at my own pace and not forcing myself to keep up with someone else.

But the reality is that we never run alone. Before his ascension into heaven, Jesus told his disciples: "And behold, I am with you always, to the close of the age" (Mt 28:20). Whether we are aware of it or not, Jesus is always with us, on our runs and in every other area of life.

When we are living in a state of grace and right relationship with God, his presence is a blessing. It gives us strength, joy, and meaning. Either way, he's there with us. In his classic spiritual autobiography *Confessions*, Saint Augustine says that God is "closer to us than we are to ourselves." There is no escaping God.

When we are living sinfully, his presence becomes uncomfortable. But this is actually a good thing. Our sin is like a pebble in our running shoe that keeps bothering us; we have to get it out in order to feel right again. Once we do, God's presence becomes comfortable again.

Remember that God is with you in every area of your life. Are you studying for a test? Struggling to pay bills? Pursuing a master's degree? Facing the death of a loved one? Wondering how to repair a relationship? Whatever the situation or circumstance, God is with you. Our good heavenly Father will never call us to run a race and then leave us to our own abilities to complete it. He remains with us, giving us advice, instruction, and encouragement. He's there on the sidelines, cheering us on as we press forward. He makes sure we have the proper nutrition and training to finish the race to the best of our ability. He is always personally invested in us.

When describing what kind of father God is, Jesus said: "Or what man of you, if his son asks him for bread, will give him a stone? Or if he asks for a fish, will give him a serpent? If you then, who are evil, know how to give good gifts to your children, how much more will your Father who is in heaven give good things to those who ask him!" (Mt 7:9–11). God is not only with us, he is rooting for us to finish the race victoriously.

The next time you go on a run, keep in mind that it's your Almighty Maker who is giving you the strength and ability to move. He is with you always, sharing your effort and your joy.

Whether it's a morning jog, a 5K, a marathon, or the race of life, we never run alone. With Saint Paul, we can boldly say: "And I am sure that he who began a good work in you will bring it to completion at the day of Jesus Christ" (Phil 1:6).

PRAY
Thank you, Lord, for being with me always. Help me remember that I never run alone.

RUN
On your run today, be mindful that God is with you. You are not alone because it is in him that you live and move and have your being (see Acts 17:28).

30
The Race Set before Us

*Do you not know that in a race all the
runners compete, but only one receives the
prize? So run that you may obtain it.*
1 Corinthians 9:24

REFLECT
Before I became Catholic, I thought of conversion as a fixed moment in time. You were lost, then you said a prayer to accept Jesus, then you were saved. Indeed, in the summer between my sophomore and junior years in high school, I had such a conversion experience at a small Baptist church in the hills of Kentucky.

I had been raised to believe in God, but my family rarely went to church, except to mark big occasions like Christmas and

Easter. But at that little church, I truly heard the Good News for the first time and understood that God is real, he is personal, and he loves me. I felt his love through the church members, total strangers who hugged me and said they loved me and were glad I was there. I had never experienced anything like it. So one summer night during the "altar call," I walked up the aisle and prayed with the pastor to receive Jesus. I'll always be grateful for that moment.

As I've grown older, though, I've come to see conversion a little differently. Rather than understanding it as one specific moment in time, I realize that it's a continuous process. I used to see salvation as the finish line: you crossed it, and the matter was settled; you were saved. Now, I see it as the starting line: you cross it, and the race has just begun.

Saint Paul urges us to persevere in running the race that lies before us, keeping our eyes fixed on Jesus. You don't need perseverance for a race that's behind you. When you commit your life to God, the race is just beginning. After all, no one becomes a Christian and then lives sin-free for the rest of their days.

As Catholics, we could say that we "get saved" every time we worthily receive the Body and Blood of Jesus at Mass. He himself said: "he who eats my flesh and drinks my blood has eternal life, and I will raise him up at the last day" (Jn 6:54). Each time we receive the Eucharist, we receive him as our Savior anew, renewing the covenant he made with us to save us.

The Race Set before Us **131**

Of course, we can encounter him outside the Mass, too. We can pray to him anywhere — in the living room, in the car, at work, or wherever we happen to be. Sometimes we mess up and fall away, but he's always waiting for us to repent and return to him. Paul said: "For the word of the cross is folly to those who are perishing, but to us who are being saved it is the power of God" (1 Cor 1:18). We aren't just saved by professing faith at one moment in time. We are being saved. Salvation is an ongoing process forever taking place.

So how does this work? Paul told the Philippians to "work out your own salvation with fear and trembling; for God is at work in you, both to will and to work for his good pleasure" (2:12–13). Yes, we have work to do. But it is God himself who gives us the desire and helps us to do the work. We are partners with him in our salvation, and it all goes back to Jesus. If he had not sacrificed himself on the cross in the first place, salvation would not be available to us.

The great thing about the spiritual race is that we can train for it even while we're running it. We can build up our strength, speed, and endurance by receiving the sacraments. We can be fueled by wisdom and inspiration from the Scriptures. We can receive encouragement and support from other believers all along the way. Maybe that's what the prophet Isaiah was hinting at when he said that "they who wait for the LORD shall renew their strength, they shall mount up with wings like eagles, / they shall run and not be weary, they shall walk and not faint" (Is 40:31).

When will the race end? None of us knows. But one day, after all our perseverance, we'll reach the finish line: heaven. Instead of encountering a race volunteer draping our necks with a finisher's medal, we'll be met and embraced by the arms of Jesus, who died for us and rose again. He will be our reward.

It's the greatest race we'll ever run.

PRAY
Dear God, thank you for making me a runner. "Forgetting what lies behind and straining forward to what lies ahead," help me "press on toward the goal for the prize of the upward call of God in Christ Jesus" (Phil 3:13–14).

RUN
Keep up the good work you have begun in using this devotional. If you are preparing for a race, all the best as you continue to train. If you're just running for fun, praise God in your movement. Today on your run, remember that each step brings you closer to your goal.

Acknowledgments

We never run — or write a book — alone. I'm thankful to all the people who made this book possible. Carol Bolton Easterly, my wife and champion. My father, Ron Easterly, who taught me the joy of running. My mother, Vicki Easterly, for her unfailing encouragement and support. All the coaches and mentors who encouraged me as a runner and a writer. My friend and mentor Barbara Nicolosi, who led me into the Catholic Church. My manager, John Bauman, who's stuck with me through the sinking and swimming seasons of my writing career. My friend and fellow runner Justine Schmiesing. My excellent editor, Mary Beth Baker. And all those friends, known and unknown, who have cheered me along the way. Thank you all!

About the Author

Chris Easterly is a professional screenwriter, independent filmmaker, and author. A graduate of the Warner Brothers Television Writers Workshop, he has written for shows on Fox, Cartoon Network, and the Hallmark Channel. Chris is a frequent contributor to the blog at CatholicMatch.com. His memoir *Falling Forward* was selected as an exclusive Amazon Kindle Single. Represented by Bauman Management in Los Angeles, he is a member of the Writers Guild of America.